WHAT ON EARTH?

TREES

Kevin Warwick
Pau Morgan

Contents

Find out why leaves change color on page 9.

Meet the trees

Branching out into poetry...4
What is a tree made of?...6
Let's look at leaves...8
Start a leaf collection...10
Create a colorful tree...12

See how to make tree shadow art on page 24.

New trees

Fallen leaves...14
From seed to tree...16
How far from home?...18
A hedge for your window...20
Needles and scales...22

Make pretty cone decorations for your home on page 32.

Trees up close

Shadow art...24
Inside and outside...26
Tree bark art...28
The mouse and the fir tree...30
Make some cone decorations...32
Pine cone weather station...34

Read about how the Douglas fir saved a mouse on page 30.

Big, tall, and old

Ancient wonders...36

How old is that tree?...38

How tall is that tree?...40

Touching the stars...42

Discover the world's oldest trees on page 36.

Find out how trees can save polar bears on page 53.

Importance of trees

Welcome guests...44

Make a tree hotel...46

Shake a tree...48

Trees around the world...50

Trees and global warming...52

Make a tree identification book...54

What do trees give us?...56

Make your own paper...58

Templates...60

Glossary...62

Index...64

Make your own paper on page 58.

Find trees with a tree identificaton book on page 54.

Branching out into poetry

Can you write a poem about the trees that are growing near you?

Rainbow Fall

Maples are red,
ash leaves turn brown,
holly leaves stay green
all year round.

Beech trees can't really
make up their mind,
for purple or green leaves
are easy to find.

Birch trees and hazel
are easy to see,
with bright yellow leaves
when they fall from the tree.

A rainbow of colors
is out in plain view,
in the leaves of the trees,
just waiting for you.

My Favorite Tree

Home for a bird,
food for a bee.
Wood for a house,
shade for me.

What is a tree made of?

Trees come in many different shapes and sizes, but they are all made up of the same parts. Each part has a special job to do.

Fruits grow around tree seeds. The seeds are protected inside the fruit until they are ready to fall from the tree and grow.

If we get the seeds from this apple, we can grow our own trees!

Leaves make food for the tree. Each leaf needs sunshine to do this.

Flowers make the seeds that will grow into new trees.

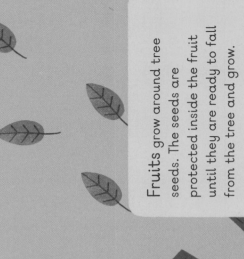
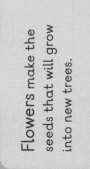

Bark is the outer layer of the tree. Its job is to protect the inside of the tree.

This woodpecker has a hard time pecking through the tough bark.

Roots act like anchors, holding the tree in place. They also take in water from the soil. Trees need water to live, just like you need it to live too!

Trunks and branches are made of wood, which is very strong. Their job is to hold the tree upright and make sure its leaves are facing the sunshine.

The wind won't blow this tree down because its roots are deep and strong.

Did you know?

Almost half of every tree is underground! Tree roots are not easy to see, but they have very important jobs to do.

Let's look at leaves

Leaves use the light from the sun to make food for trees. This process is called photosynthesis.

Sunlight gives the leaves the energy they need to change **carbon dioxide** and water into food.

Oxygen is a gas that is released through the process of **photosynthesis**. This is good for humans because we need **oxygen** to breathe.

Carbon dioxide is a gas in the air that gets inside the leaf through tiny holes in the leaf surface.

Sugar is also made during photosynthesis and is food for trees. It moves to all the other parts of the tree.

Water travels all the way from the roots to the leaf. Most of the water leaves the leaf through **evaporation**.

Hooray for trees!

What Happens?

Photosynthesis is possible because of something inside the leaf called **chlorophyll**. Chlorophyll uses energy from sunlight to help the leaf mix the water and carbon dioxide together to make sugar.

All shapes and sizes

Leaves come in different shapes and sizes, but they are usually green. This is because leaves contain chlorophyll, which is green in color.

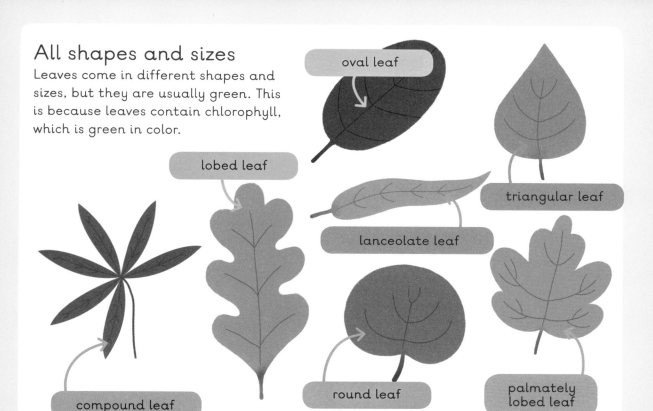

oval leaf

triangular leaf

lobed leaf

lanceolate leaf

compound leaf

round leaf

palmately lobed leaf

Leaves can turn red, yellow, orange, and even purple in the fall!

Did you know?

Trees drop their leaves when it's cold, but before they do they use up all of their chlorophyll. When the green chlorophyll is gone, the autumn leaves turn many different colors.

Start a leaf collection

Collect and keep leaves in a scrapbook. How many types of leaves can you find?

Tool kit
- roll of paper towels
- two pieces of letter-size cardboard
- collected leaves
- two heavy books
- sticky tape
- scrapbook

What to do

1 Layer four sheets of paper towel on top of one of the pieces of cardboard.

2 Place some leaves on top of the paper towels. Make sure the leaves are flat and spread out so they are not touching each other.

You can press more than one layer of leaves, but you will need to use more paper towels and add more books on top.

Did you know?
Leaves are mostly made of water! If you want to keep them for a long time, you need to make sure that they are completely dry.

3 Layer four more sheets of paper towel on top of the leaves. Put another piece of cardboard on top of the paper towels.

4 Put two heavy books on top of the cardboard.

5 Store it in a warm place for about three weeks.

6 When the leaves are dry, take them out gently and carefully tape them into your scrapbook.

Try this...
Collect different leaves during each season and organize your scrapbook into four sections with one for spring, summer, fall, and winter.
Your collection will show how leaves change during the year.

Create a colorful tree

Use real leaves to make a colourful model of a tree.

Tool kit

- collected leaves
- tracing paper
- colored pencils
- scissors
- 11 in x 17 in paper
- glue
- template tree (p. 60)

What to do

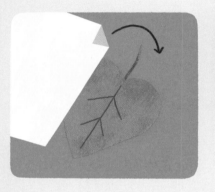

1 Place a leaf on a table. Lay a sheet of tracing paper on top of the leaf and hold it in place firmly.

2 Gently rub a colored pencil over the tracing paper. Use the flat edge to make it easier.

3 Be sure to rub over the whole leaf and just past the edges of the leaf.

4 Lift the tracing paper off and carefully cut out the leaf shape you've just drawn. Repeat until you have a selection of leaves in different colors and shapes.

5 Use the template tree to draw a tree onto the 11 in x 17 in paper, so that it fills the paper, and color it in.

6 Glue your cut-out leaf shapes onto the branches of the tree shape to finish your colorful tree.

I made a fall tree. I love the colors at this time of year.

My tree is special because it is made up of different shapes and colors!

Try this...

You can make a specific type of tree by using the same shape and color for every leaf, or you can use different colors and shapes to make a unique tree!

Fallen leaves

Can you match each tree
to its fallen leaf?

In the fall hazel trees make hazelnuts, which are very tasty.

The bark of willow trees has been used for healing and pain relief for centuries around the world.

Holly is an **evergreen** tree with prickly leaves that do not fall off the tree in the winter.

Maple syrup is made from the sugar maple tree, which grows in North America. The maple leaf is on the Canadian flag.

The wood from oak trees was used to make big wooden ships for sailing far out to sea.

Many birch trees have white bark that peels off like paper and can be used to make canoes!

From seed to tree

Without animals or wind, trees wouldn't be able to make seeds and no new trees would grow.

Making seeds

To make seeds, the flowers on a tree need **pollen**. The pollen must be carried from one part of a flower to another part of a different flower. This is called **pollination**.

Sometimes insects carry pollen from one flower to another.

Insects like big, colorful flowers the most.

These flowers don't need to attract insects, so they aren't colorful.

Sometimes the wind can blow the pollen through the air to another flower.

16

Seed Dispersal

Once the seeds are made they need to travel far away from the tree, so that they have space to grow. This is called **seed dispersal.** Trees disperse their seeds in a number of different ways.

Whee! Winged seeds have wings that help them travel far away on the wind.

Some seeds grow inside tasty fruits. Birds eat the fruits and fly away. The seeds drop to the ground in their poop later.

Squirrels carry acorns far away. They bury them to eat later, but often forget where!

Did you know?

It is the pollen in the wind that makes you sneeze if you have hay fever.

Now, where should I bury this acorn?

How far from home?

How far do you think different types of seeds will travel? Test them in this scientific experiment.

Tool kit

- different tree seeds with wings
- different tree seeds without wings
- record table (like the one below)
- measuring tape
- an adult to help

What to do

Which seed type will travel the farthest when it drops from a tree?

I predict this seed will travel the farthest because it has wings.

Seed number	Winged/ Not winged	Distance traveled
1	NW	1 ft
2	W	3 ft
3	NW	
4	NW	
5	NW	
6	W	
7	W	
8	W	

1. Look at your seeds and make a **prediction**. Which seed do you think will travel the farthest and why?

2. Fill out the boxes on your record table with what you know and write your prediction at the top.

3 Ask your adult to help you find a safe high place to drop your seeds from. Drop a seed and ask someone to mark where it lands.

4 Measure the distance along the ground from where you dropped the seed to where it landed. Write this number on your record table.

5 Compare the **data** for all your seeds. Which seed type traveled the farthest?

What happens?
Winged seeds spin around, keeping them in the air longer. This makes it more likely that a gust of wind will catch them, so they can travel further away from the tree.

A hedge for your window

Plant your very own hedge to decorate your window. Care for it and watch it grow.

Tool kit
- egg carton
- scissors
- gloves
- soil (or potting soil)
- spray bottle
- collected tree seeds

What to do

1 Cut the lid off the egg carton.

Wear gloves when handling any soil.

2 Put soil in each egg hole so that they are almost full, then spray with water.

3 Place five seeds in each egg hole. Cover with more soil and spray with more water.

4 Store your egg carton in a warm place for a few weeks. Spray water on the soil in the morning and evening.

Now that the trees are starting to grow, they need lots of sunshine!

Did you know?
Seeds need warmth and water to start growing, but they don't need any light until they start to poke out of the soil.

5 When the trees start poking through the soil, move them to the windowsill so they have light to grow.

Make sure you keep the soil moist so the trees always have water to drink.

Try this...
Watch your hedge get taller and thicker. After it has been growing for a few weeks, you can trim the leaves with scissors to give the hedge a shape you like. But only cut off small pieces at a time.

Needles and scales

Many trees have wide, flat leaves. They are called **broadleaf** trees. There is another group of trees called **conifers**, which look very different!

Needles

The leaves of many conifers are called **needles** because that is what they look like. They are long and thin, and they often have pointy tips.

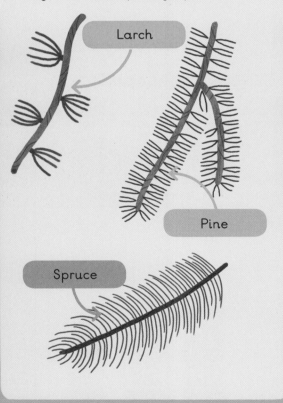

Larch

Pine

Spruce

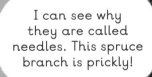

I can see why they are called needles. This spruce branch is prickly!

22

Scales

The leaves of some conifers are short and flattened. They look like the **scales** on a fish or a snake.

Cypress

Arborvitae

Cedar

Look at the pretty patterns on this cedar tree. They look like feathers.

This larch tree is not dead. It has just dropped its needles for the winter. It is deciduous!

Did you know?

Sometimes conifers are called evergreen trees. This is because they don't drop their needles or scales in the winter and they stay green all year round. Be careful, though. You might get fooled! Some conifers are **deciduous trees** and they do drop their needles in the winter.

Shadow art

Find trees in the sunshine to discover what their shadows reveal.

Tool kit

- clipboard
- paper
- pencil
- colored pencils

What to do

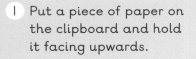

1 Put a piece of paper on the clipboard and hold it facing upwards.

2 Walk around the trees and look at the shadows of the branches and leaves on your paper.

3 Stop when you like the shapes of the shadows. Use your pencil to trace the outline of the shapes on your paper. Then color the shapes in.

4 Move to another position and look for new shapes to draw on another piece of paper.

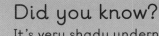

Did you know?

It's very shady underneath trees, but some light gets through. If you walk under trees on a sunny day, you will see patches of light and many shadows. The shadows make interesting shapes.

Try this...
Look for shadows at the same place in the morning and afternoon. See how the shadows and patterns on your paper change as the day goes by.

Remember to never look directly at the sun. It is very bad for your eyes.

This tree's shadow makes pretty patterns.

What happens?
The position of the sun in the sky changes throughout the day, causing the sunlight to come through the trees from different angles. As the day goes on, the shadows you see around the tree will change and so will the patterns you see on your paper, even if you stay in the same place.

Inside and outside

Let's take a close look at the trunk of a tree.

Trees can grow big and tall because their trunks and branches are made of wood.

Wood

Wood is made up of **cells**. Each wood cell is long and hollow. They are very small but there are millions of them in a tree. These cells are all held tightly together with a very sticky glue-like substance. This means that wood is very strong!

Did you know?

Because wood cells are hollow, wood is like millions of tiny straws all glued together. This is very useful for the tree. Water from the roots moves through these hollow cells, all the way up to the leaves.

The bark on the outside of the tree is also made up of many small cells. Bark cells are shaped like bricks and they are solid.

Bark

Trees are constantly making more **bark** cells. These cells push tightly together around the outside of the wood and make a wall that nothing can get through. Sometimes the bark gets very thick to help the tree stay warm in the cold winter. Thick bark also protects the wood from the heat of a forest fire.

NO ENTRY

Trees need their bark. Don't peel it off!

Did you know?

There are a lot of insects that want to eat trees. There are also a lot of diseases that can make trees sick. Even a small hole in the bark can let a disease or insect wriggle inside.

Tree bark art

Discover the many different types of tree bark by using them for drawings.

Tool kit

- letter-size paper
- paint roller and tray (or a rolling pin with a towel wrapped around it)
- acrylic or poster paint
- colored pencils

What to do

This tree has long, wiggly grooves in its bark that look like waves.

Try not to tear the paper while you are rolling.

1 Hold a piece of paper against a tree with one hand. See if you can find trees with different types of bark.

2 Cover the roller with paint and gently roll it up and down over the paper. You will get an imprint of the bark on the paper.

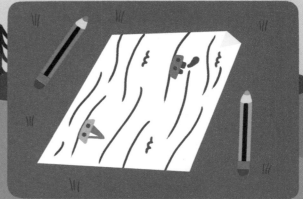

3 Take the paper down from the tree and find a flat place to do your drawing.

4 Draw around the shapes made by the bark imprints on the paper. Add color with the colored pencils.

Try this...
After you have rolled the paper once, turn it on its side and roll it again. You will get even more interesting imprints to trace.

I have used the bumps and swirls on this bark to make stars in the night sky.

The up-and-down cracks on this bark make good outlines for roads for cars.

Did you know?
Bark cells are not stretchy, so as the tree grows wider, the bark splits. This is what makes cracks and patterns in bark.

The mouse and the fir tree

The Douglas fir lives along the northwestern coast of North America. This story is told by the people of this area and explains how this tree came to look the way it does.

A long time ago there was an old forest next to the sea. Many different kinds of trees lived in this forest, but one stood out above the rest. While the other trees liked to talk to each other and play in the wind, the Douglas fir stood quietly, keeping watch over the forest.

One hot, dry summer, a forest fire started. The animals in the forest fled to safety, but one little mouse could not run fast enough to escape.

So she went from tree to tree asking for shelter.

First, she asked the big maple tree.

Please, Maple, can you help me?

"No," said the maple tree, "I won't survive this fire and can't help you."

Next, the mouse went to the cedar tree.

The cedar said, "No. I, too, won't survive this fire and can't help you."

Please, Cedar, can you help me?

The little mouse ran from tree to tree but no one would help her, until she asked the Douglas fir.

Please, Douglas fir, can you help me?

Yes, little mouse, I can help you. My thick bark will protect us from the flames.

The little mouse climbed into the Douglas fir's branches and hid under the scales of a cone. Many other mice followed her. The fire passed and the great Douglas fir stood tall over what was left of the forest.

Eventually new trees grew, the animals returned, and the forest lived on. And, if you look closely at the cones of a Douglas fir tree, you can see the tail and back feet of the little mouse hiding under the scales.

Can you write your own story about a tree that you like?

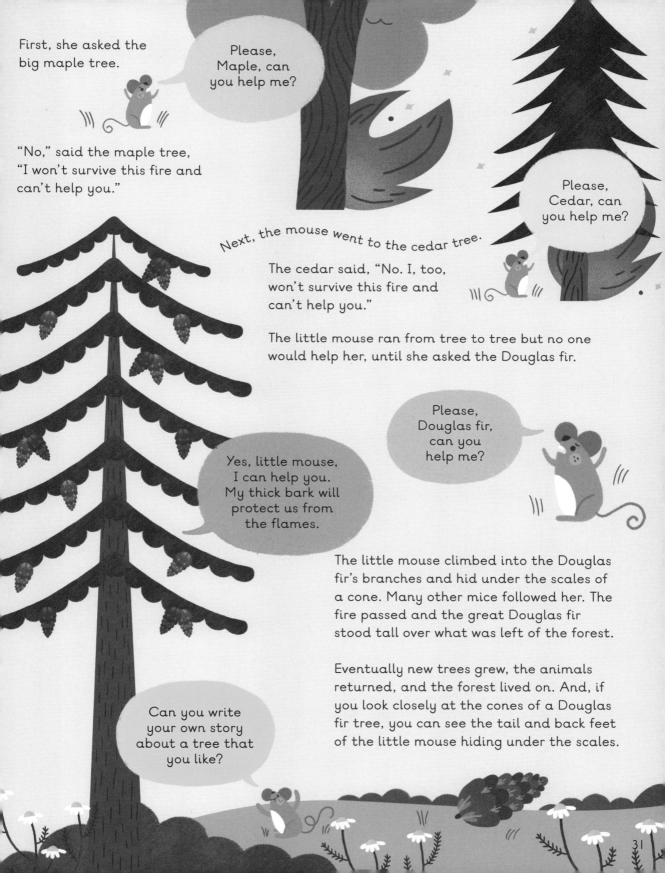

31

Make some cone decorations

Use some color and your imagination to turn conifer cones into decorations for your home.

Tool kit

- collected cones
- paint and paintbrush
- glue
- glitter
- ribbon

What to do

1 Collect lots of different cones. Look on the ground under trees but also on branches.

2 Place the cones in a warm place to dry for about a week.

3 Use paint, glitter, and your imagination to decorate the cones.

4 Tie a ribbon around the base of each cone. Hang them up to decorate your home.

Did you know?

Conifer trees don't make fruit to hold their seeds like an apple tree does. Instead, conifers protect their seeds in cones. These cones have lots of overlapping scales that are stiff and usually brown in color. There are many different shapes and sizes of cones and they make good decorations.

Pine

Cypress

Larch

I made a table decoration with my pinecones.

Try this...

Try different ways of coloring your cones: paint them all the same color or paint each scale a different color. You could even spread some glue on the cones and sprinkle glitter on them to make the cones sparkle.

Pine cone weather station

See if you can predict the weather by using just a pinecone!

Tool kit
- pine cone
- poster tack or modeling clay

What to do

Any of these cones will make a good weather station.

1 Find a large cone. Pinecones work best for this weather station, but you can use any large conifer cone.

2 Put some poster tack on the bottom of the cone.

3 Put the cone on an outside window sill so that you can see it from inside your home.

4 Push the cone down so the poster tack keeps it firmly in place.

5 Watch your cone closely from day to day. Look for changes in the shape and size of the cone.

What happens?

When the weather is sunny, the scales of the cone shrink and open up so that the seeds can escape. The seeds can then be blown far away to find a new space to grow. In rainy weather, the scales of the cone close tightly so the seeds can't escape. This is because if any seeds escaped in the rain, they would fall close to the tree and have no space to grow.

Ancient wonders

The oldest person in the world lived to the age of 122 years! Can you guess the age of the oldest tree in the world?

Name: Giant Sequoia
Home: United States
Age: about 3,200 years

Name: Kauri
Home: New Zealand
Age: about 2,000 years

Name: Olive
Home: Greece
Age: about 3,500 years

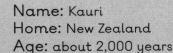

For some trees, 122 years would be old. But for many trees, this is a very young age indeed!

Oldest tree in the world
In California, there is a forest of ancient pine trees. One of these has reached the age of almost 5,000 years. That is 40 times as old as the oldest person!

Name: Yew
Home: Wales
Age: about 4,200 years

Name: Cypress
Home: Iran
Age: about 4,000 years

Did you know?
Surprisingly, most of the oldest trees are not very big. Tall, straight trees usually get cut down so that their wood can be used. They don't get a chance to grow old. The really old trees are often small and crooked.

Sometimes old trees need help from sticks, just like my grandfather!

How old is that tree?

Find out how old the trees around you are by using these simple tricks.

Tree rings

Trees grow a new layer of wood every year, which creates **tree rings**. The rings can be seen on a tree stump or a cut branch, and you can count them to work out how old the tree is.

Tool kit

- magnifying glass
- different color push pins
- measuring tape
- record table (template on p. 61)

What to do

1 Method one: find a tree that has been cut down, or a branch that has been cut off a tree.

2 Look closely with the magnifying glass and count the rings, starting from the outside.

3 Put some push pins in the tree rings at special years for you.

Tree hugs

Trees grow about ¾in (2cm) in **circumference** every year. So you can estimate the age of a tree without having to cut it down by measuring around the tree.

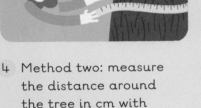

4 Method two: measure the distance around the tree in cm with the measuring tape.

5 Write the measurement in your record table as the circumference for Tree 1.

6 Divide the circumference by two. Write this number in the record table for the age of Tree 1.

The circumference of this tree is 200cm.

Wow! That means the tree is about 100 years old.

Try this...

Work with your friends to measure 10 trees and fill up your record table. For big trees, you will need to get a friend to help you by holding one end of the measuring tape while you walk around the tree with the other end.

How tall is that tree?

It is easy to measure how tall you are, but how do you measure a tree when the top is so high up?

Tool kit
- a stick
- measuring tape

What to do

1 Find a stick that is the same length as the distance between your chin and the end of your fingers.

2 Hold the bottom of the stick, keeping your arm and the stick straight. This makes a triangle shape with two sides of equal length.

4 Keep moving back until the tree looks the same size as the stick. Stop and put the stick on the ground by your feet.

3 Walk backward from the tree you are measuring. Stop every few steps to look and compare the length of the stick you're holding with the tree.

What happens?

You have made a larger triangle shape with your tree as one side of the triangle. We know the two sides of the small triangle are the same size. If you measure the distance between the stick and the tree you can figure out the height of the tree, because it will be the same.

Try this...

Measure the height of different size trees with your friends. Compare your results and see if they are the same.

This tree is 92ft tall. That's taller than my house!

I got the same height when I measured the tree!

Touching the stars

Trees are some of the biggest living things on the planet. Just look at how big some of them can be!

The tallest tree in the world is a **coast redwood**, 380 ft (115 m), in California. It is about as tall as 36 school buses stacked on top of each other.

The Australian mountain ash, 327 ft (100 m), is the tallest tree in Australia. It is as tall as a soccer field is long!

The Statue of Liberty in New York City is 305 ft (93 m) tall.

Try this...
Find the height of the trees by using the ruler. Compare the heights of the trees with the heights of the famous buildings mentioned on this page.

130m

120 m

110 m

100m

90m

80m

Welcome guests

Over time, trees become homes for lots of animals and other plants.

Birds build their nests in high branches.

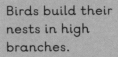

Ivy grows around tree trunks.

Deer like the shelter and protection that trees give.

Mosses often grow on the tree bark.

It is safe and warm here, and there is plenty for me to eat.

Did you know?
In the northern **hemisphere**, moss usually grows on the north side of tree trunks. So a tree is like a compass with the moss pointing north.

Squirrels stay in branches for safety, and to find nuts and seeds to eat.

If we take care of this one tree, we are also taking care of all these other plants and animals as well!

Some birds, like woodpeckers, dig holes in the tree trunk. They make holes to find insects to eat and they make holes to build their nests in.

Many different types of insects and spiders live on trees. They are looking for food and for places to hide.

Mushrooms grow at the foot of trees. Earthworms and insects live on the ground, or underground among the roots.

Happy homes

Trees make happy and safe homes for many living things. They provide food to eat, shelter from the weather, and places to hide from danger. This makes trees a good **habitat** for both plants and animals. A single tree can be home to hundreds of types of plants and animals!

Make a tree hotel

Use different parts of trees to attract animal visitors to your backyard.

Tool kit

- gloves
- tree leaves, twigs, branches, and logs
- large pieces of cardboard
- clear tape

What to do

Wear gloves when collecting leaves and wood.

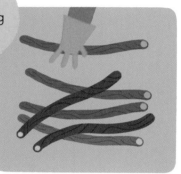

1. The hotel will have four rooms. Collect leaves and pile them near the edge of your backyard to make the Leaf Room.

2. Collect small twigs and place them in a pile next to the leaves to make the Twig Room.

3. Find larger sticks or branches on the ground. Don't break branches from trees. Make a pile of these to make the Branch Room.

4. Find some small logs. Make a pile of these to make the Log Room.

You can use pieces of firewood if you can't find logs.

Try this...

Give your hotel a name. Make a sign out of cardboard and write your hotel name on it. Tape the sign to a twig and stick it in the ground near your hotel. You could make signs with names for each room as well.

LEAF
ROOM

THE
OAK INN

TWIG
ROOM

Watch closely

Keep watch over your hotel to see who is visiting. The best times to see visitors are when you get up in the morning and just before you go to bed at night.

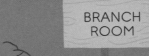

BRANCH
ROOM

LOG
ROOM

What happens?

The different piles of tree materials which make up your hotel create new habitats. These provide shelter and food to many different animals. So your hotel will increase the **biodiversity** of your backyard.

Shake a tree

You might be surprised to see who is living on the branches of the trees around you.

Tool kit

- light colored sheet (not fluffy material)
- gloves
- paintbrush
- clear plastic cup
- magnifying glass

What to do

Wear gloves when shaking the tree, and watch out for thorns!

1 Find a tree branch that you can easily reach.

2 Spread the sheet under the branch.

3 Shake and tap the branch firmly, but gently.

Be careful not to break the branch, and make sure no one is nearby when you shake it.

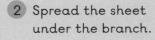

4 Look closely at the sheet to see what's there.

What happens

Insects and spiders like to hide out of sight in trees. By shaking the branch, you knock them out of their hiding places. Insects with wings will fly away, so look quickly to see these. The others will crawl around on the sheet for you to see.

5 Use the paintbrush to gently sweep some of the insects into a cup. Now you can look at them closely with the magnifying glass. Can you count the number of different types of creatures you find?

6 When you've finished, the insects you found will want to go home. Be gentle with them and put them back at the base of the tree.

Time for the insects to go home.

Trees around the world

Travel around the world and visit some special trees.

The sugar maple tree grows in **Canada** and **New England**. The broadleaf forests here are some of the most colorful in the world in the fall.

It rains a lot on the Pacific coast of **North America**, making it the best habitat for the world's tallest trees.

The Amazon rain forest in **South America** has the highest biodiversity of any forest in the world. Many different trees grow here.

The monkey puzzle tree grows in central **Chile**. It has sharp, triangular leaves and even monkeys can't climb it.

N

The Major Oak in Sherwood Forest, England, is believed to have been home to Robin Hood and his merry men many years ago.

The Crooked Forest in Poland is a group of pine trees that are all curved at the base. No one knows why they are this shape.

The Chapel Oak in France is hollow in the middle and has a church built inside it. It has an upstairs and downstairs, and people attend services on Sundays.

The boreal forest is the largest forest in the world. It is made up of conifers and it covers most of Russia, northern Canada, and northern Europe.

The Lost Tree is an acacia tree. It stands alone in the Sahara Desert in Africa.

The baobab tree is a common tree in Madagascar.

The Gloucester Tree is a karri tree in Australia. It has a ladder built into its trunk and, if you are brave, you can climb up 190ft (60m), to the top.

Trees and global warming

The temperature of the air around Earth is rising, and this is causing lots of problems. Trees can come to the rescue and help stop this.

Global warming
Cars and factories release gases and other harmful substances when they burn fuel.

The gases are called **greenhouse gases**. They sit in the **atmosphere**, acting like the glass of a greenhouse.

The sun's rays can easily pass through the greenhouse gases and warm Earth.

Carbon dioxide is a greenhouse gas.

But the heat from the Earth cannot escape back up through the gases, just like heat cannot escape through the glass in a greenhouse. It is trapped, and this makes the temperature rise.

Trees to the rescue

Trees can help get rid of the greenhouse gases in the air. Carbon dioxide is a greenhouse gas and trees use carbon dioxide for photosynthesis. By planting more trees, we can help slow down **global warming** and keep our planet happy.

Remember: trees take in carbon dioxide and release oxygen, which is good for us and the planet!

The heat from Earth can now escape back into space. The temperature does not rise.

When there are lots of trees growing there will be fewer greenhouse gases.

Did you know?

Planting trees can help polar bears! Global warming is melting a lot of ice on the ocean near the North Pole. This means that polar bears can't get to their food. Planting trees helps keep the temperature from going up, so the polar bears still have plenty of ice to walk on.

Make a tree identification book

Sometimes even experts find trees they don't recognize. When they do, they use identification books to help them identify the tree.

Tool kit
- five sheets of letter-size paper
- Two pieces of letter-size cardboard
- colored pencils
- 6in ruler
- hole puncher
- ribbon

What to do

1 Find five different types of trees to make fact sheets for.

2 Write the name for each tree at the top of each fact sheet. Ask an adult to help.

3 Take a leaf from the tree and draw a picture of it on the fact sheet. Color the drawing the same color as the leaf.

4 Measure the size of the leaf and mark the size on your drawing.

5 Look closely at the leaf. Write down any other features you can see.

This round leaf is almost 6 in wide. Look! It's round and covered with small hairs.

Decorate the cover of your book with colorful drawings of trees or leaves.

6 Punch holes in the sheets and the cardboard. Tie them all together with the ribbon, using the cardboard to make a front and back cover.

Try this...
Test your friends. Take them to the trees in your fact sheets and see if they can use your book to identify the trees.

What do trees give us?

Look around you. How many of the things that you see every day come from trees?

Food
We get a lot of yummy things to eat from trees, including fruits and nuts, and maple syrup for pancakes. Yum!

Wood
The wood in the trunk and branches is cut up and used to make many useful things, such as houses, ships, furniture, and firewood.

Paper
Books, newspapers, and the paper you write on are made from the wood of trees.

Arts and crafts

Trees inspire creativity! We can use cones for painting, leaves for rubbings, and branches for wreaths.

Trees also give us things to play with, like strong branches for a tree house...

...a swing,

...or even just shade on a hot day.

Did you know?

There are people called foresters who manage our forests. When we cut down trees for important wood products, foresters plant new trees to replace them.

Make your own paper

Use recyclable materials to make your own colorful paper.

Tool kit

- scrap paper or cardboard
- food blender
- an adult to help
- waxed paper
- dish towels
- rolling pin
- scissors

What to do

Use old newspapers, writing paper, or even cardboard egg cartons. Don't use anything shiny or waxy.

1 Tear the recyclable materials into small pieces. Put them into the blender with water and leave to soak for 20 minutes.

2 Ask an adult to help you blend the mixture into a smooth pulp.

3 Place a sheet of waxed paper on a dish towel and then scoop the pulp onto it.

Try this...

You can make your paper more fun by stirring in food coloring or flower petals after the pulp is made.

4 Place another sheet of waxed paper on top of the pulp. Use a rolling pin to flatten the pulp into a thin layer.

5 Carefully peel the waxed paper off. Your pulp is now a sheet of new paper.

6 Lay a dry dish towel on top of the wet sheet of new paper. Gently roll over the dish towel to soak up water from the sheet.

It might take a few days to dry completely.

The paper is now ready for writing or drawing.

7 Carefully peel the dish towel off. Place your new paper in a warm place to dry.

8 Carefully peel your new sheet of paper from the waxed paper. Use the scissors to trim it to the size and shape you want.

Templates

How old is that tree record table

Tree number	Location of tree	Circumference of tree (centimeters)	Estimated age of tree (circumference divided by 2)
1			
2			
3			
4			
5			
6			
7			
8			
9			
10			

How tall is that tree record table

Tree number	Location of tree	Height of tree (length between stick and foot of tree)
1		
2		
3		
4		
5		
6		
7		
8		
9		
10		

Glossary

Atmosphere The mixture of gases which make up the air around Earth.

Bark The thick, protective outer layer of a tree.

Biodiversity The number of different types of plants and animals that live in an area.

Broadleaf tree A type of tree with wide, flat leaves.

Carbon dioxide A gas in the air around Earth that trees use to make their food. It also causes global warming.

Chlorophyll A chemical in leaves that takes in energy from the sun to make food. Chlorophyll gives leaves their green color.

Cells All living things are made up of cells. Cells are very small and they come in many shapes. They pack together to make the bodies of plants and animals.

Circumference The distance measured around the outside of a circular shape.

Conifer A tree whose leaves look like needles or scales and usually stay on the tree all year round.

Data Numbers that you get from measuring something in an experiment

Deciduous tree A tree that loses its leaves in the winter.

Evaporation The process of liquid turning into a gas.

Evergreen tree A tree that holds on to its leaves all year long and does not lose them in the winter.

Global warming The slow rise in Earth's average temperature.

Greenhouse gas A gas in the air around Earth that causes global warming. Greenhouse gases let sunshine through but keep the heat from escaping back into space.

Habitat The home of a plant or animal, where it can find shelter and food.

Hemisphere Half of a round shape. Earth can be divided into a northern and southern hemisphere, or into an eastern and western hemisphere.

Needle A type of leaf that looks like a needle and is found on coniferous trees.

Oxygen A gas in the air around Earth that we need to breathe. Trees produce oxygen when they make their food.

Photosynthesis This is how leaves use the sun's energy to make food. Sugar is made by combining water and carbon dioxide gas.

Pollen A yellow powder made by male flowers. It is made up of millions of tiny particles called pollen grains.

Pollination When pollen is moved from one part of a flower to another part of a flower to make a new seed.

Prediction A guess about what will happen in the future.

Scales Small flat leaves that look like scales and grow on coniferous trees.

Seed dispersal The movement of new seeds away from the plant where they were made so that the new plants have enough space to grow.

Tree rings The rings on the inside of a tree that are created by growth.

Index

acorns 17
age of a tree 36–39
animal and plant habitats 44–49
arborvitae 23
ash 4, 42
bark 7, 15, 26, 27
beech 4
biodiversity 47, 50
birch 4, 15
branches 7, 26, 48, 57
broadleaf trees 22, 50
carbon dioxide 8, 52, 53
cedar 23, 31
cells 26, 27, 29
chlorophyll 8, 9
cones 31, 32–35
conifers 22–23, 33, 51
cypress 23, 33, 37
deciduous trees 23
decorations 32–33
diseases 27

Douglas fir 30, 31, 43
evergreen trees 15, 23
flowers 6, 16
food for trees 6, 8
foresters 57
fruits and nuts 6, 15, 17, 56
global warming 52–53
greenhouse gases 52, 53
hazel 4, 15
hedge 20–21
height 40–43
holly 4, 15
identification book 54–55
larch 22, 23, 33
leaf collection 10–11
leaves 6, 8–15, 22, 26
maple 4, 15, 31, 50
model of a tree 12–13
needles and scales 22, 23, 31, 33, 35
oldest trees 36–37
oxygen 8, 53

paper-making 58–59
parts of a tree 6–7
photosynthesis 8, 53
pine 22, 33, 37, 51
poems 4–5
pollen and pollination 16, 17
roots 7
seed dispersal 17–19
seeds 6, 16–19, 20, 21, 33, 35
spruce 22
stories 30–31
sunlight 8, 25
tree art 24–25, 28–29
tree hotel 46–47
tree products 15, 56–57
tree rings 38
trunks 7, 26–27
water 8, 10, 26
weather station 34–35
willow 15
wood 15, 26, 37, 38, 56
world, trees in the 50–51

Quarto Knows

Quarto is the authority on a wide range of topics.

Quarto educates, entertains and enriches the lives of our readers—enthusiasts and lovers of hands-on living.

www.quartoknows.com

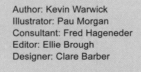

Author: Kevin Warwick
Illustrator: Pau Morgan
Consultant: Fred Hageneder
Editor: Ellie Brough
Designer: Clare Barber

© 2018 Quarto Publishing plc

First Published in 2018 by QEB Publishing, an imprint of The Quarto Group.
6 orchard Road
suite 100
Lake Forest, CA 92630
T: +1 949 380 7510
F: +1 949 380 7575
www.QuartoKnows.com

A CIP record for this book is available from the Library of Congress.

ISBN 978 1 68297 305 9

9 8 7 6 5 4 3 2 1

Manufactured in Dongguan, China TL102017

FSC
www.fsc.org

MIX
Paper from responsible sources
FSC® C104723